MAD LIBS®

PEACE, LOVE, AND MAD LIBS

By Roger Price and Leonard Stern

Mad Libs
An Imprint of Penguin Random House

MAD LIBS
Penguin Young Readers Group
An Imprint of Penguin Random House LLC

Mad Libs format and text copyright © 2009 by Penguin Random House LLC.
All rights reserved.

Concept created by Roger Price & Leonard Stern

Published by Mad Libs,
an imprint of Penguin Random House LLC,
345 Hudson Street, New York, New York 10014.
Printed in the USA.

ISBN 9780843189308
27 29 30 28 26

MAD●LIBS®
INSTRUCTIONS

MAD LIBS® is a game for people who don't like games! It can be played by one, two, three, four, or forty.

• RIDICULOUSLY SIMPLE DIRECTIONS

In this tablet you will find stories containing blank spaces where words are left out. One player, the READER, selects one of these stories. The READER does not tell anyone what the story is about. Instead, he/she asks the other players, the WRITERS, to give him/her words. These words are used to fill in the blank spaces in the story.

• TO PLAY

The READER asks each WRITER in turn to call out a word—an adjective or a noun or whatever the space calls for—and uses them to fill in the blank spaces in the story. The result is a MAD LIBS® game.

When the READER then reads the completed MAD LIBS® game to the other players, they will discover that they have written a story that is fantastic, screamingly funny, shocking, silly, crazy, or just plain dumb—depending upon which words each WRITER called out.

• EXAMPLE (*Before* and *After*)

"_____!" he said _____
    EXCLAMATION   ADVERB

as he jumped into his convertible _____ and
                                            NOUN

drove off with his _____ wife.
                            ADJECTIVE

"_____*Ouch*_____!" he said _____*Stupidly*_____
    EXCLAMATION   ADVERB

as he jumped into his convertible _____*cat*_____ and
                                            NOUN

drove off with his _____*brave*_____ wife.
                            ADJECTIVE

MAD LIBS®
QUICK REVIEW

In case you have forgotten what adjectives, adverbs, nouns, and verbs are, here is a quick review:

An ADJECTIVE describes something or somebody. *Lumpy*, *soft*, *ugly*, *messy*, and *short* are adjectives.

An ADVERB tells how something is done. It modifies a verb and usually ends in "ly." *Modestly*, *stupidly*, *greedily*, and *carefully* are adverbs.

A NOUN is the name of a person, place, or thing. *Sidewalk*, *umbrella*, *bridle*, *bathtub*, and *nose* are nouns.

A VERB is an action word. *Run*, *pitch*, *jump*, and *swim* are verbs. Put the verbs in past tense if the directions say PAST TENSE. *Ran*, *pitched*, *jumped*, and *swam* are verbs in the past tense.

When we ask for A PLACE, we mean any sort of place: a country or city (*Spain*, *Cleveland*) or a room (*bathroom*, *kitchen*).

An EXCLAMATION or SILLY WORD is any sort of funny sound, gasp, grunt, or outcry, like *Wow!*, *Ouch!*, *Whomp!*, *Ick!*, and *Gadzooks!*

When we ask for specific words, like a NUMBER, a COLOR, an ANIMAL, or a PART OF THE BODY, we mean a word that is one of those things, like *seven*, *blue*, *horse*, or *head*.

When we ask for a PLURAL, it means more than one. For example, *cat* pluralized is *cats*.

MAD LIBS® is fun to play with friends, but you can also play it by yourself! To begin with, DO NOT look at the story on the page below. Fill in the blanks on this page with the words called for. Then, using the words you have selected, fill in the blank spaces in the story.

Now you've created your own hilarious MAD LIBS® game!

PEACE IS THE WORD

NOUN _____

NUMBER _____

PLURAL NOUN _____

COLOR _____

NOUN _____

NOUN _____

NOUN _____

PERSON IN ROOM _____

VERB (PAST TENSE) _____

NOUN _____

ADJECTIVE _____

PART OF THE BODY (PLURAL) _____

ADJECTIVE _____

NOUN _____

PLURAL NOUN _____

PLURAL NOUN _____

MAD LIBS®

PEACE IS THE WORD

Our _____ Studies teacher had us write a/an
           NOUN

_____-word paper on the different symbols for peace.
    NUMBER

I learned many interesting _____, such as:
                      PLURAL NOUN

* The _____ dove is a symbol of love, peace, and
          COLOR

_____.
   NOUN

* The olive _____ represents a peace offering or
             NOUN

goodwill gesture, as in: *The next-door neighbors extended a/an*

_____ *branch to* _____ *after their*
     NOUN   PERSON IN ROOM

dog _____ *on his/her* _____.
     VERB (PAST TENSE)   NOUN

* The "V" sign is a/an _____ gesture made by
                ADJECTIVE

holding up two _____ in the shape of the
          PART OF THE BODY (PLURAL)

letter *V*.

* The peace sign is one of the most _____ symbols
                ADJECTIVE

in the _____. It was popular with hippies, who
     NOUN

spray-painted it on _____ while shouting, "Give
          PLURAL NOUN

_____ a chance!"
   PLURAL NOUN

MAD LIBS® is fun to play with friends, but you can also play it by yourself! To begin with, DO NOT look at the story on the page below. Fill in the blanks on this page with the words called for. Then, using the words you have selected, fill in the blank spaces in the story.

Now you've created your own hilarious MAD LIBS® game!

THE HIPPIE SHACK

PART OF THE BODY _____

ADJECTIVE _____

NOUN _____

PLURAL NOUN _____

PLURAL NOUN _____

NOUN _____

ARTICLE OF CLOTHING _____

NOUN _____

PART OF THE BODY _____

ADJECTIVE _____

ADJECTIVE _____

NOUN _____

PLURAL NOUN _____

PART OF THE BODY _____

VERB ENDING IN "ING" _____

NOUN _____

ADJECTIVE _____

MAD LIBS®

THE HIPPIE SHACK

Are you a hippie wannabe? If so, visit the Hippie Shack. They'll

outfit you from head to _____ in the colorful,
                          PART OF THE BODY

_____ clothing worn by those _____-loving
ADJECTIVE   NOUN

flower _____ of the '60s! We suggest starting with
       PLURAL NOUN

basic bell-bottom _____, preferably a vintage pair with
                  PLURAL NOUN

_____-shaped patches sewn over the holes. Then select
NOUN

any _____ with fringe, tie-dye, or a psychedelic
    ARTICLE OF CLOTHING

_____ pattern. You can accessorize to your
NOUN

_____'s content! We have some _____belts
PART OF THE BODY   ADJECTIVE

and _____ jewelry with the peace _____
    ADJECTIVE   NOUN

prominently displayed. Or you can wear strings of beaded

_____, and we have scarves that wrap around
PLURAL NOUN

your _____. Trust us, when you step out of the
     PART OF THE BODY

_____ room in your cool new threads, you'll
VERB ENDING IN "ING"

not only look like a groovy _____, you'll feel pretty
                            NOUN

_____, too!
ADJECTIVE

From PEACE, LOVE, AND MAD LIBS® • Copyright © 2009 by Penguin Random House LLC.

MAD LIBS® is fun to play with friends, but you can also play it by yourself! To begin with, DO NOT look at the story on the page below. Fill in the blanks on this page with the words called for. Then, using the words you have selected, fill in the blank spaces in the story.

Now you've created your own hilarious MAD LIBS® game!

HAPPENING

VERB _____

NUMBER _____

ADJECTIVE _____

ADJECTIVE _____

NOUN _____

ADJECTIVE _____

PLURAL NOUN _____

A PLACE _____

ADJECTIVE _____

PLURAL NOUN _____

PERSON IN ROOM _____

ANIMAL (PLURAL) _____

VERB ENDING IN "ING" _____

TYPE OF FOOD (PLURAL) _____

NOUN _____

ADJECTIVE _____

NOUN _____

VERB _____

NOUN _____

MAD LIBS®

HAPPENING

Run, don't _____, to join _____ of your
             VERB   NUMBER

closest friends at the greatest _____ outdoor musical
                                        ADJECTIVE

experience of our _____ generation. This once-
                           ADJECTIVE

in-a/an-_____ event is guaranteed to provide a/an
                NOUN

_____ weekend filled with music, peace, love,
      ADJECTIVE

and _____ in the picturesque setting of (the)
           PLURAL NOUN

_____. Bands such as the _____
      A PLACE   ADJECTIVE

_____, _____ and the _____,
  PLURAL NOUN   PERSON IN ROOM   ANIMAL (PLURAL)

the _____ _____, and many more will be
    VERB ENDING IN "ING"   TYPE OF FOOD (PLURAL)

rocking the _____ all night long! This _____
             NOUN   ADJECTIVE

happening will take place rain or _____, so
                               NOUN

_____ accordingly. It's sure to be a legendary
      VERB

_____!
      NOUN

MAD LIBS® is fun to play with friends, but you can also play it by yourself! To begin with, DO NOT look at the story on the page below. Fill in the blanks on this page with the words called for. Then, using the words you have selected, fill in the blank spaces in the story.

Now you've created your own hilarious MAD LIBS® game!

WORLD PEACE...AND OTHER PROMISES

ADJECTIVE _____

ADJECTIVE _____

PERSON IN ROOM _____

PLURAL NOUN _____

ADJECTIVE _____

ADVERB _____

ADJECTIVE _____

PLURAL NOUN _____

NOUN _____

PLURAL NOUN _____

TYPE OF LIQUID _____

NOUN _____

ADJECTIVE _____

ADVERB _____

PLURAL NOUN _____

PLURAL NOUN _____

PLURAL NOUN _____

NOUN _____

PERSON IN ROOM _____

ADJECTIVE _____

MAD LIBS®

WORLD PEACE . . . AND OTHER PROMISES

Our school is voting for this year's ______________ [ADJECTIVE] president! Let's listen in as the ______________ [ADJECTIVE] candidate, ______________ [PERSON IN ROOM], makes his/her final campaign speech:

"My fellow ______________ [PLURAL NOUN]: I know the ______________ [ADJECTIVE] changes you want and ______________ [ADVERB] deserve. If elected, I promise to put an end to ______________ [ADJECTIVE] homework and pop ______________ [PLURAL NOUN]. I will expand the lunch menu to include ______________ [NOUN]-burgers and cheese-stuffed ______________ [PLURAL NOUN]. I will fill every drinking fountain with chocolate ______________ [TYPE OF LIQUID]. I will see to it that the only acceptable exercise in gym class is dodge-______________ [NOUN]. Finally, for every ______________ [ADJECTIVE] student in detention, I ______________ [ADVERB] swear to make video ______________ [PLURAL NOUN], comic ______________ [PLURAL NOUN], and widescreen ______________ [PLURAL NOUN] available in the detention ______________ [NOUN]. So remember: A vote for ______________ [PERSON IN ROOM] today is a vote for a/an ______________ [ADJECTIVE] school tomorrow!"

From PEACE, LOVE, AND MAD LIBS® • Copyright © 2009 by Penguin Random House LLC.

MAD LIBS® is fun to play with friends, but you can also play it by yourself! To begin with, DO NOT look at the story on the page below. Fill in the blanks on this page with the words called for. Then, using the words you have selected, fill in the blank spaces in the story.

Now you've created your own hilarious MAD LIBS® game!

HAPPY CAMPERS

ADJECTIVE _____

ADJECTIVE _____

ADJECTIVE _____

PLURAL NOUN _____

PLURAL NOUN _____

ADJECTIVE _____

NOUN _____

VERB ENDING IN "ING" _____

NOUN _____

ARTICLE OF CLOTHING (PLURAL) _____

NOUN _____

PLURAL NOUN _____

TYPE OF LIQUID _____

VERB ENDING IN "ING" _____

ADJECTIVE _____

NOUN _____

MAD LIBS®
HAPPY CAMPERS

When life gets too _____, there's no better antidote than
ADJECTIVE

to forget the _____ grind and go camping with some
ADJECTIVE

_____ friends. With the moon and _____
ADJECTIVE   PLURAL NOUN

twinkling overhead and the sound of _____ chirping
PLURAL NOUN

in the woods, sitting around the campfire and singing a/an

_____ chorus or two of "She'll Be Coming 'Round the
ADJECTIVE

_____" or "I've Been _____ on the Railroad"
NOUN   VERB ENDING IN "ING"

is a great way to restore peace to your inner _____.
NOUN

Or, if you choose, you can scare the _____ off
ARTICLE OF CLOTHING (PLURAL)

everyone with _____ stories. You can also just
NOUN

sit quietly, toasting _____ and sipping mugs of
PLURAL NOUN

steaming _____ before snuggling into your
TYPE OF LIQUID

_____ bag. Yes, there's nothing better than the
VERB ENDING IN "ING"

_____ outdoors to guarantee a good night's
ADJECTIVE

_____!
NOUN

MAD LIBS® is fun to play with friends, but you can also play it by yourself! To begin with, DO NOT look at the story on the page below. Fill in the blanks on this page with the words called for. Then, using the words you have selected, fill in the blank spaces in the story.

Now you've created your own hilarious MAD LIBS® game!

FOR PEACE SAKE!

ADJECTIVE _____

PLURAL NOUN _____

VERB ENDING IN "ING" _____

PART OF THE BODY (PLURAL) _____

NOUN _____

PLURAL NOUN _____

ADVERB _____

NOUN _____

VERB _____

PLURAL NOUN _____

NUMBER _____

PART OF THE BODY (PLURAL) _____

PLURAL NOUN _____

ADJECTIVE _____

NOUN _____

MAD☺LIBS®
FOR PEACE SAKE!

My _____ brother and sister are at it again, fighting
　　　　ADJECTIVE

like cats and _____. I've had enough. I've decided to
　　　　　　　　PLURAL NOUN

give them a stern _____ to. I will look them straight in
　　　　　　　　VERB ENDING IN "ING"

their _____ and say, "Living under the same
　　　PART OF THE BODY (PLURAL)

_____ means we're going to get on one another's
　　　　NOUN

_____ from time to time, but you two are being
　　PLURAL NOUN

_____ insensitive! You don't have to argue at the
　　　　ADVERB

drop of a/an _____. Think before you
　　　　　　　　NOUN

_____. Take a few deep _____ and
　　　VERB　　　　　　　　　　　　　　　　　PLURAL NOUN

count to _____. If you don't, I'm warning
　　　　　NUMBER

you, I'll take matters into my own _____ and
　　　　　　　　　　　　　　PART OF THE BODY (PLURAL)

knock you flat on your _____! Now let's have some
　　　　　　　　　PLURAL NOUN

_____ peace and _____."
　　ADJECTIVE　　　　　　　　　NOUN

MAD LIBS® is fun to play with friends, but you can also play it by yourself! To begin with, DO NOT look at the story on the page below. Fill in the blanks on this page with the words called for. Then, using the words you have selected, fill in the blank spaces in the story.

Now you've created your own hilarious MAD LIBS® game!

FAR-OUT FOOD

ADJECTIVE _____

PART OF THE BODY _____

NOUN _____

NUMBER _____

ADJECTIVE _____

ADJECTIVE _____

NOUN _____

ADJECTIVE _____

PLURAL NOUN _____

ADJECTIVE _____

PLURAL NOUN _____

NOUN _____

ADVERB _____

NOUN _____

NOUN _____

PLURAL NOUN _____

PART OF THE BODY _____

ADJECTIVE _____

MAD LIBS®

FAR-OUT FOOD

Welcome to the Far-Out Café! Our _____ diner

ADJECTIVE

serves _____-lickin' good eats that are out of this

PART OF THE BODY

_____. Our most popular dishes are:

NOUN

- **Hippie Hamburger**: _____ oz. of _____

NUMBER — ADJECTIVE

  beef on a/an _____ bun, stacked with sprouts, tomato,

ADJECTIVE

  and a/an _____ slice

NOUN

- **Flower Child Chicken**: This _____ dish is served

ADJECTIVE

  with wild _____ and homegrown _____

PLURAL NOUN — ADJECTIVE

  vegetables on a bed of flower _____

PLURAL NOUN

- **Groovy Grilled Cheese**: Sharp _____ cheese melted

NOUN

  between two slices of _____ baked _____,

ADVERB — NOUN

  served with _____ chips

NOUN

- **Psychedelic Salad**: On a bed of dark leafy _____, an array

PLURAL NOUN

  of creative exuberances that will tempt your _____

PART OF THE BODY

  and provide a/an _____ meal in itself

ADJECTIVE

MAD LIBS® is fun to play with friends, but you can also play it by yourself! To begin with, DO NOT look at the story on the page below. Fill in the blanks on this page with the words called for. Then, using the words you have selected, fill in the blank spaces in the story.

Now you've created your own hilarious MAD LIBS® game!

A LITTLE PEACE & QUIET

NOUN _____

NOUN _____

PLURAL NOUN _____

NOUN _____

NOUN _____

PLURAL NOUN _____

NOUN _____

ADVERB _____

PLURAL NOUN _____

PLURAL NOUN _____

PLURAL NOUN _____

PLURAL NOUN _____

PART OF THE BODY (PLURAL) _____

PLURAL NOUN _____

PLURAL NOUN _____

PLURAL NOUN _____

NOUN _____

MAD LIBS®

A LITTLE PEACE & QUIET

What would happen if you fell overboard from a/an

_____ and washed up on a deserted tropical
    NOUN

_____? Here's a list of survival _____:
    NOUN   PLURAL NOUN

• The human _____ requires one thing more than all
                    NOUN

others to survive: _____. Without water, you would only
                        NOUN

last for a few _____. So you'd have to find a source of fresh
                  PLURAL NOUN

running _____ and boil it before _____ drinking it.
              NOUN   ADVERB

• Look for plants, _____, and insects to eat. You can also
                        PLURAL NOUN

try leaves, berries, roots, and even the bark of some _____.
                                                            PLURAL NOUN

• Food can also be hunted with primitive _____. Use rocks,
                                                PLURAL NOUN

sticks, ropes, _____, or anything else you can get your
                  PLURAL NOUN

_____ on.
PART OF THE BODY (PLURAL)

• Gather _____ for a campfire. Rub two _____
              PLURAL NOUN   PLURAL NOUN

together until a fire is created. You will have warmth and a way to

cook and boil your _____. Perhaps most importantly,
                        PLURAL NOUN

you'll have a way to signal a passing _____.
                                            NOUN

MAD LIBS® is fun to play with friends, but you can also play it by yourself! To begin with, DO NOT look at the story on the page below. Fill in the blanks on this page with the words called for. Then, using the words you have selected, fill in the blank spaces in the story.

Now you've created your own hilarious MAD LIBS® game!

EVERYONE NEEDS A GOOD FRIEND

ADVERB _____

NOUN _____

ADJECTIVE _____

ADJECTIVE _____

ADJECTIVE _____

PLURAL NOUN _____

COLOR _____

PLURAL NOUN _____

VERB _____

NOUN _____

NOUN _____

PLURAL NOUN _____

MAD LIBS®
EVERYONE NEEDS
A GOOD FRIEND

As a Greek philosopher _____ once said, "One good

ADVERB

_____ makes a poor man rich." Here are some

NOUN

important qualities to look for in a/an _____ friend:

ADJECTIVE

• Whether you're right or _____, your friend will be

ADJECTIVE

there for you—through thick and _____.

ADJECTIVE

• When you are down in the _____ and feeling

PLURAL NOUN

_____, your friend will tell you funny _____

COLOR   PLURAL NOUN

to make you _____ with laughter.

VERB

• When you don't have a/an _____ to wear, your friend

NOUN

should generously offer you their favorite _____ so

NOUN

you can look like a million _____.

PLURAL NOUN

MAD LIBS® is fun to play with friends, but you can also play it by yourself! To begin with, DO NOT look at the story on the page below. Fill in the blanks on this page with the words called for. Then, using the words you have selected, fill in the blank spaces in the story.

Now you've created your own hilarious MAD LIBS® game!

PEACE, LOVE, AND POETRY

PLURAL NOUN _____

PERSON IN ROOM _____

VERB _____

NOUN _____

PLURAL NOUN _____

ADJECTIVE _____

PLURAL NOUN _____

NOUN _____

COLOR _____

PART OF THE BODY _____

VERB _____

NOUN _____

PLURAL NOUN _____

ADVERB _____

A PLACE _____

PEACE, LOVE, AND POETRY

"Peace, Love, and the Pursuit of _____"
_____PLURAL NOUN

by _____
___PERSON IN ROOM

Teach everyone you meet to _____ in perfect harmony,
_____VERB

Reach out and embrace a friend or _____, or go hug a tree!
_____NOUN

Preach to _____, both big and _____, to
_____PLURAL NOUN_____ADJECTIVE

give peace a chance,

And stop and smell the _____, or do a little dance.
_____PLURAL NOUN

Love your neighbors, love your friends, love your _____,
_____NOUN

too—

And love the good ol' USA—the red, the _____, and the blue!
_____COLOR

Extend your _____ in friendship to everyone you meet.
_____PART OF THE BODY

Invite a stranger to _____, or bring a stray _____
_____VERB_____NOUN

home to eat.

These random acts of _____ will put a smile on a face,
_____PLURAL NOUN

And they'll _____ transform (the) _____
_____ADVERB_____A PLACE

into a better place!

MAD LIBS® is fun to play with friends, but you can also play it by yourself! To begin with, DO NOT look at the story on the page below. Fill in the blanks on this page with the words called for. Then, using the words you have selected, fill in the blank spaces in the story.

Now you've created your own hilarious MAD LIBS® game!

TIE-DYE FOR FASHION

ADJECTIVE _____

ADJECTIVE _____

NOUN _____

ADJECTIVE _____

NOUN _____

PLURAL NOUN _____

PLURAL NOUN _____

PART OF THE BODY (PLURAL) _____

NOUN _____

ADJECTIVE _____

NUMBER _____

TYPE OF LIQUID _____

NOUN _____

ADJECTIVE _____

PART OF THE BODY (PLURAL) _____

MAD LIBS®

TIE-DYE FOR FASHION

Tie-dying is a/an _____ way to dye your clothing so
                        ADJECTIVE

you can look like a/an _____ hippie. Here are some
                              ADJECTIVE

instructions for tie-dying your own _____:
                                          NOUN

1. Select a/an _____ article of clothing and use
                    ADJECTIVE

   _____ bands to tie it into different sections.
         NOUN

2. Prepare your dye according to the _____ on the
                                          PLURAL NOUN

   package.

3. Remember to put on a pair of rubber _____
                                              PLURAL NOUN

   over your _____ to protect them as you dip the
                 PART OF THE BODY (PLURAL)

   _____ into the dye.
         NOUN

4. For _____ results, keep the material in the dye for
            ADJECTIVE

   at least _____ minutes. Then remove and rinse under cold
                  NUMBER

   running _____.
                TYPE OF LIQUID

5. Hang on a/an _____ outside to dry.
                      NOUN

6. Wear it and enjoy the _____ looks on people's
                                ADJECTIVE

   _____.
         PART OF THE BODY (PLURAL)

MAD LIBS® is fun to play with friends, but you can also play it by yourself! To begin with, DO NOT look at the story on the page below. Fill in the blanks on this page with the words called for. Then, using the words you have selected, fill in the blank spaces in the story.

Now you've created your own hilarious MAD LIBS® game!

YOUR GOOD FORTUNE

PERSON IN ROOM (FEMALE) _____

NOUN _____

VERB _____

PART OF THE BODY _____

NOUN _____

PLURAL NOUN _____

PERSON IN ROOM (MALE) _____

CELEBRITY (MALE) _____

NOUN _____

A PLACE _____

ADJECTIVE _____

ADVERB _____

PLURAL NOUN _____

VERB ENDING IN "ING" _____

ADJECTIVE _____

ADJECTIVE _____

ADJECTIVE _____

PART OF THE BODY (PLURAL) _____

NOUN _____

MAD LIBS®

YOUR GOOD FORTUNE

When I entered the room, Madame _____, the
_____PERSON IN ROOM (FEMALE)

famous _____-teller, gestured for me to _____.
_____NOUN _____VERB

"What do you wish to know?" she asked as she prepared to read my

_____. "Will I marry a handsome _____?"
PART OF THE BODY _____NOUN

I asked. She replied, "Yes. Two _____ named
_____PLURAL NOUN

_____ and _____ think you are
PERSON IN ROOM (MALE) _____CELEBRITY (MALE)

the prettiest, smartest _____ in all of (the)
_____NOUN

_____. Only one will make you truly _____,
A PLACE _____ADJECTIVE

so you must choose _____." "Will I be successful?"
_____ADVERB

I asked. "You will find fame and _____ with
_____PLURAL NOUN

your _____ skills," she responded. "But will
_____VERB ENDING IN "ING"

I be happy?" "Yes, you will always be surrounded by a/an

_____ family and _____ friends who will
ADJECTIVE _____ADJECTIVE

put you on a/an _____ pedestal and worship at your
_____ADJECTIVE

_____." _Wow_, I thought. _All that and she hasn't_
PART OF THE BODY (PLURAL)

used her crystal _____ _yet!_
_____NOUN

MAD LIBS® is fun to play with friends, but you can also play it by yourself! To begin with, DO NOT look at the story on the page below. Fill in the blanks on this page with the words called for. Then, using the words you have selected, fill in the blank spaces in the story.

Now you've created your own hilarious MAD LIBS® game!

HALL MONITOR

PERSON IN ROOM _____

NOUN _____

ADJECTIVE _____

NOUN _____

VERB ENDING IN "ING" _____

ADJECTIVE _____

ADJECTIVE _____

NOUN _____

NOUN _____

ADJECTIVE _____

ARTICLE OF CLOTHING _____

VERB ENDING IN "ING" _____

NOUN _____

TYPE OF FOOD _____

PLURAL NOUN _____

VERB _____

NOUN _____

MAD LIBS®

HALL MONITOR

My name is _____. I'm the _____ monitor and
          PERSON IN ROOM   NOUN

peacekeeper here at _____ _____ Memorial
                  ADJECTIVE   NOUN

School. It's my duty to keep the students _____
                                   VERB ENDING IN "ING"

through the halls in a/an _____ and orderly fashion.
                       ADJECTIVE

Originally, I wasn't sure I was _____ enough for
                            ADJECTIVE

this job. I'm not the strongest _____ in school, and
                            NOUN

I don't claim to be the smartest _____, either. But
                            NOUN

I have the _____ ability to sense that someone has
              ADJECTIVE

something up his _____. So heed this warning: If
               ARTICLE OF CLOTHING

you're thinking about _____ in the hallways without
                        VERB ENDING IN "ING"

a/an _____ pass or planning to start an all-out
        NOUN

_____ fight in the cafeteria, forget about it. I have
     TYPE OF FOOD

_____ in the back of my head. You can run, but
     PLURAL NOUN

you can't _____, and you'll be in the principal's
            VERB

_____ in no time flat.
     NOUN

MAD LIBS® is fun to play with friends, but you can also play it by yourself! To begin with, DO NOT look at the story on the page below. Fill in the blanks on this page with the words called for. Then, using the words you have selected, fill in the blank spaces in the story.

Now you've created your own hilarious MAD LIBS® game!

FAMOUS HIPPIES IN HISTORY

ADJECTIVE _____

A PLACE _____

VERB _____

PLURAL NOUN _____

PERSON IN ROOM (MALE) _____

ADJECTIVE _____

PLURAL NOUN _____

ADJECTIVE _____

PLURAL NOUN _____

PERSON IN ROOM (FEMALE) _____

PLURAL NOUN _____

ADJECTIVE _____

ADJECTIVE _____

PLURAL NOUN _____

NOUN _____

PERSON IN ROOM (FEMALE) _____

NOUN _____

PLURAL NOUN _____

ADJECTIVE _____

NOUN _____

MAD LIBS®
FAMOUS HIPPIES
IN HISTORY

The hippie lifestyle may be a thing of the past, but many

_____ hippies made (the) _____ a better place
   ADJECTIVE   A PLACE

in which to live, work, and _____. Here's a look at a few
                                   VERB

of those _____ of the 1960s:
         PLURAL NOUN

- **Barefoot** _____ was a/an _____
             PERSON IN ROOM (MALE)   ADJECTIVE

  songwriter who wrote about love and _____.
                                     PLURAL NOUN

  His _____ music inspired millions of _____
        ADJECTIVE   PLURAL NOUN

  everywhere.

- **Crazy Daisy** _____ was known for weaving
             PERSON IN ROOM (FEMALE)

  beautiful _____ into her hair. This _____
       PLURAL NOUN   ADJECTIVE

  flower child also painted many _____ murals
                         ADJECTIVE

  depicting _____ living in peace and _____.
       PLURAL NOUN   NOUN

- **Grandma Groovy Pants** _____ was an anti-
                      PERSON IN ROOM (FEMALE)

  _____ activist who championed equality for all
   NOUN

  _____ in our society and supported her _____
   PLURAL NOUN   ADJECTIVE

  beliefs by marching for justice and _____.
                          NOUN

MAD LIBS® is fun to play with friends, but you can also play it by yourself! To begin with, DO NOT look at the story on the page below. Fill in the blanks on this page with the words called for. Then, using the words you have selected, fill in the blank spaces in the story.

Now you've created your own hilarious MAD LIBS® game!

THE SUMMER OF LOVE LETTERS, PART 1

PLURAL NOUN _____

ADJECTIVE _____

PLURAL NOUN _____

ADJECTIVE _____

ADJECTIVE _____

ADVERB _____

PLURAL NOUN _____

ADJECTIVE _____

PART OF THE BODY _____

ADVERB _____

A PLACE _____

ADJECTIVE _____

NOUN _____

PLURAL NOUN _____

ADJECTIVE _____

ADJECTIVE _____

PERSON IN ROOM (FEMALE) _____

MAD LIBS®
THE SUMMER OF LOVE LETTERS, PART 1

I was in the attic going through some old _____ when,
PLURAL NOUN

to my _____ surprise, I came across my parents' old love
ADJECTIVE

_____. Here's one of Mom's most _____
PLURAL NOUN   ADJECTIVE

letters:

My _____ Hippie Man,
ADJECTIVE

I miss you _____—more than _____
ADVERB   PLURAL NOUN

can say! I miss your _____ smile. I miss the way my
ADJECTIVE

_____ beats when your eyes stare _____
PART OF THE BODY   ADVERB

into mine. I miss going for long walks at (the) _____
A PLACE

at sunset. Do you ever picture us spending the rest of our

_____ lives together? I do. I dream of our living in a
ADJECTIVE

cozy house with a picket _____. I know in my heart of
NOUN

_____ that I want to grow _____ with you.
PLURAL NOUN   ADJECTIVE

With all my _____ love,
ADJECTIVE

_____
PERSON IN ROOM (FEMALE)

MAD LIBS® is fun to play with friends, but you can also play it by yourself! To begin with, DO NOT look at the story on the page below. Fill in the blanks on this page with the words called for. Then, using the words you have selected, fill in the blank spaces in the story.

Now you've created your own hilarious MAD LIBS® game!

THE SUMMER OF LOVE LETTERS, PART 2

ADJECTIVE _____

ADJECTIVE _____

PLURAL NOUN _____

NOUN _____

PLURAL NOUN _____

ADJECTIVE _____

PART OF THE BODY _____

PART OF THE BODY _____

NOUN _____

PART OF THE BODY _____

NOUN _____

PART OF THE BODY _____

NOUN _____

SILLY WORD _____

NOUN _____

ADVERB _____

NOUN _____

PERSON IN ROOM (MALE) _____

MAD LIBS®
THE SUMMER OF LOVE LETTERS, PART 2

Now, here's a/an _____ letter from my _____
                ADJECTIVE   ADJECTIVE

dad to my mom:

To the girl of my _____,
                 PLURAL NOUN

Not a/an _____ goes by that I don't think of you.
            NOUN

I don't know what I did to deserve you, but I thank my lucky

_____ that I am so _____ to be the one who
    PLURAL NOUN   ADJECTIVE

holds the key to your _____. I dreamed last night that I
                    PART OF THE BODY

asked your father for your _____ in marriage. With a/an
                        PART OF THE BODY

_____ on his face, he nodded his _____ and
    NOUN   PART OF THE BODY

said, "Yes." When I awakened, I realized I don't want to wait until I

graduate from _____ school. I want to come home now,
                 NOUN

drop down on one _____, put a diamond _____
                PART OF THE BODY   NOUN

on your finger, and pop the question. When you say "_____"
                                     SILLY WORD

you'll make me the happiest _____ in the world.
                         NOUN

Truly, madly, _____ in love with you,
               ADVERB

Your _____-to-be, _____
      NOUN   PERSON IN ROOM (MALE)

MAD LIBS® is fun to play with friends, but you can also play it by yourself! To begin with, DO NOT look at the story on the page below. Fill in the blanks on this page with the words called for. Then, using the words you have selected, fill in the blank spaces in the story.

Now you've created your own hilarious MAD LIBS® game!

TEAM PEACE

NOUN _____

PLURAL NOUN _____

ADJECTIVE _____

PERSON IN ROOM _____

PLURAL NOUN _____

ADJECTIVE _____

PLURAL NOUN _____

ADJECTIVE _____

VERB _____

ADJECTIVE _____

PLURAL NOUN _____

NOUN _____

ADJECTIVE _____

ADJECTIVE _____

ADJECTIVE _____

PART OF THE BODY _____

NOUN _____

ADJECTIVE _____

MAD LIBS®
TEAM PEACE

It was the day of the most important _____ on the schedule

NOUN

and the coach knew his team was a bundle of _____.

PLURAL NOUN

He wisely invited the _____ Guru _____

ADJECTIVE   PERSON IN ROOM

to help his players find their inner _____.

PLURAL NOUN

The Guru's pep talk was simple and _____:

ADJECTIVE

Block out the screaming _____ in the stadium. Focus on

PLURAL NOUN

becoming one with the _____ ball. The most important

ADJECTIVE

thing is to believe you can _____ better today than you

VERB

have in any other _____ game this season. The opposing

ADJECTIVE

_____ will try to shake your _____, but

PLURAL NOUN   NOUN

you must stay calm, cool, and _____, and always be

ADJECTIVE

positive. If one of your teammates makes a/an _____

ADJECTIVE

play, give him a/an _____ pat of encouragement on the

ADJECTIVE

_____. Now put your _____ faces on and

PART OF THE BODY   NOUN

go make us _____!

ADJECTIVE

MAD LIBS® is fun to play with friends, but you can also play it by yourself! To begin with, DO NOT look at the story on the page below. Fill in the blanks on this page with the words called for. Then, using the words you have selected, fill in the blank spaces in the story.

Now you've created your own hilarious MAD LIBS® game!

GARAGE BAND DEBUT

TYPE OF LIQUID _____

PART OF THE BODY _____

NOUN _____

ADJECTIVE _____

PART OF THE BODY (PLURAL) _____

PLURAL NOUN _____

NOUN _____

ADJECTIVE _____

COLOR _____

PERSON IN ROOM _____

PERSON IN ROOM _____

ADVERB _____

ADJECTIVE _____

NUMBER _____

ADVERB _____

PLURAL NOUN _____

PART OF THE BODY _____

NOUN _____

ADJECTIVE _____

MAD LIBS®

GARAGE BAND DEBUT

As the lights dimmed, I could feel beads of _____ drip
                                                    TYPE OF LIQUID

down my _____. The school dance was my band's
            PART OF THE BODY

first real _____ and I was so _____, I was sure
                NOUN   ADJECTIVE

everyone could see my _____ shaking. "Hello,
                            PART OF THE BODY (PLURAL)

_____!" I shouted into the micro-_____.
     PLURAL NOUN   NOUN

"We're really happy to be here at your _____ dance.
                                              ADJECTIVE

Tonight, our first song will be '_____ Haze.'" I glanced
                                        COLOR

back at _____ on keyboards and _____
              PERSON IN ROOM   PERSON IN ROOM

on drums (both of whom were sweating _____), took
                                              ADVERB

a/an _____ breath, and began the count: "And a one,
            ADJECTIVE

and a two, and a one, two, _____!" The next thing I
                                  NUMBER

knew, the audience was cheering _____ and dancing
                                        ADVERB

like _____. Even the principal was tapping his
           PLURAL NOUN

_____ on the _____. Who knows? A
   PART OF THE BODY   NOUN

school dance tonight—maybe a/an _____ record deal
                                        ADJECTIVE

tomorrow!

MAD LIBS® is fun to play with friends, but you can also play it by yourself! To begin with, DO NOT look at the story on the page below. Fill in the blanks on this page with the words called for. Then, using the words you have selected, fill in the blank spaces in the story.

Now you've created your own hilarious MAD LIBS® game!

DID YOU EVER HAVE ONE OF THOSE DAYS?

ADJECTIVE _____

NOUN _____

ADJECTIVE _____

VERB ENDING IN "ING" _____

NUMBER _____

ADJECTIVE _____

NOUN _____

NOUN _____

LETTER OF THE ALPHABET _____

ADJECTIVE _____

ADJECTIVE _____

EXCLAMATION _____

NOUN _____

MAD LIBS®
DID YOU EVER HAVE ONE OF THOSE DAYS?

Dear Diary: What a/an _____ day! I forgot my gym
ADJECTIVE

_____, so the _____ teacher made
NOUN   ADJECTIVE

me do one hundred _____ jacks. I was late getting
VERB ENDING IN "ING"

to homeroom and the teacher had me write _____
NUMBER

times, "I promise not to be _____ ever again." As if
ADJECTIVE

that's not enough, I was in the bathroom and dropped my report

in the _____! I can't turn in a soaking wet
NOUN

_____, so I'm probably going to get a/an
NOUN

_____. Did I mention someone spilled a bowl of
LETTER OF THE ALPHABET

_____ soup all over me at lunch? And worse
ADJECTIVE

than that, I bit into an apple and cracked the filling in my

_____ molar. _____! I guess I just got
ADJECTIVE   EXCLAMATION

up on the wrong side of the _____ this morning.
NOUN

MAD LIBS® is fun to play with friends, but you can also play it by yourself! To begin with, DO NOT look at the story on the page below. Fill in the blanks on this page with the words called for. Then, using the words you have selected, fill in the blank spaces in the story.

Now you've created your own hilarious MAD LIBS® game!

HIPPIE SPEAK, PART 1

ADJECTIVE _____

PLURAL NOUN _____

PERSON IN ROOM _____

NOUN _____

NUMBER _____

ADJECTIVE _____

PERSON IN ROOM _____

ADJECTIVE _____

PART OF THE BODY _____

PLURAL NOUN _____

PLURAL NOUN _____

ADJECTIVE _____

ADJECTIVE _____

VERB (PAST TENSE) _____

A PLACE _____

MAD LIBS®

HIPPIE SPEAK, PART 1

In addition to their distinctive style of dressing, hippies had their

own _____ language. Here are some of the most popular
_____ADJECTIVE_____

_____:
PLURAL NOUN

- **Groovy** meant cool. *That _____ is one groovy _____!*
  PERSON IN ROOM   NOUN

- **Far out** was _____ times better than groovy. *My mom's*
  NUMBER

  letting me go to the _____ concert with _____.
  ADJECTIVE   PERSON IN ROOM

  Far out!

- To **dig it** meant to understand. *When my teacher asked if I*

  understood the _____ homework, I nodded my
  ADJECTIVE

  _____ and said, "I dig it."
  PART OF THE BODY

- **Threads** referred to clothing. *"Man, between her peace sign*

  _____ and her tie-dyed _____, she's got
  PLURAL NOUN   PLURAL NOUN

  really _____ threads!"
  ADJECTIVE

- If something was **a gas**, it meant you had a really _____
  ADJECTIVE

  time. *It was a gas when we _____ with our friends*
  VERB (PAST TENSE)

  at (the) _____.
  A PLACE

MAD LIBS® is fun to play with friends, but you can also play it by yourself! To begin with, DO NOT look at the story on the page below. Fill in the blanks on this page with the words called for. Then, using the words you have selected, fill in the blank spaces in the story.

Now you've created your own hilarious MAD LIBS® game!

HIPPIE SPEAK, PART 2

NOUN _____

PERSON IN ROOM _____

ADJECTIVE _____

ADJECTIVE _____

NOUN _____

A PLACE _____

NOUN _____

ADJECTIVE _____

ADJECTIVE _____

PERSON IN ROOM _____

ADJECTIVE _____

NOUN _____

ADJECTIVE _____

PLURAL NOUN _____

PART OF THE BODY (PLURAL) _____

NOUN _____

MAD☺LIBS®

HIPPIE SPEAK, PART 2

- Your **pad** was your home, or the place where you hung your

  _____. *Let's go hang out at* _____*'s pad and*

NOUN · PERSON IN ROOM

  listen to some _____ *be-bop.*

ADJECTIVE

- To **crash** meant to sleep. *You look* _____. *Why don't you*

ADJECTIVE

  go in the bedroom and crash on the _____?

NOUN

- When you **split**, you left (the) _____. *As soon as the*

A PLACE

  _____ *rang, we split from school and went shopping*

NOUN

  for _____ *threads.*

ADJECTIVE

- **The scene** referred to a place where something _____

ADJECTIVE

  was going on. If _____ *is in the principal's office, it*

PERSON IN ROOM

  must be a/an _____ *scene.*

ADJECTIVE

- **Happening** described a place where every _____ *was*

NOUN

  having fun. Between the _____ *music and the delicious*

ADJECTIVE

  _____, *that party was happening!*

PLURAL NOUN

- **Peace out** meant good-bye. *He held up two* _____

PART OF THE BODY (PLURAL)

  as he left the _____ *and said, "Peace out."*

NOUN

Join the millions of Mad Libs fans
creating wacky and wonderful
stories on our apps!

Download Mad Libs today!